BIRDS OF SAGE AND SCREE

Original Paintings by Greg McHuron

Text by Bert Raynes

GRANDVIEW PUBLISHING
· Jackson, Wyoming ·

GRANDVIEW PUBLISHING
· Jackson, Wyoming ·

www.KenThomasma.com
P.O. Box 2863, Jackson, Wyoming 83001-2863

First Edition Published 2010

Standard Edition: ISBN-13: 978-1-880114-36-0

Limited Edition: ISBN-13: 978-1-880114-35-3

Library of Congress Control Number: 2010923892

Book Design: Steven J. Epstein/Dream Farm, LLC

Publisher: Peter L. Ward, tetontectonics.org

Printed in China via Global Interprint, Inc., globalinterprint.com

Portrait of Greg McHuron by Randal M. Dutra, randaldutra.com

Portrait of Bert Raynes by Kathy Robertson, treasuresiseek.com

This book was set in *Mrs. Eaves,* designed by Zuzana Licko. It is based on the font *Baskerville.*

Table of Contents

Preface

Bert's proposal that we work jointly on putting together a book, utilizing our varied backgrounds but similar philosophical ideas, was both terrifying and at the same time exhilarating. (And has been a wonderful opportunity and pleasure for me). Working with a list supplied by Bert of birds that habituate scree slopes or sagebrush flats was very challenging. It was my desire to unite animals with birds, both of which exist within the same ecology but representing the birds and habitat in full color, and at the same time indicating the presence of other inhabitants. I wanted to show a spiritual relationship between these two different types of animals and at the same time involve the viewer in a way that we all become aware of each other. This is not a book for positive bird identification, similar to Peterson's or Sibley's, but to represent the physical, spiritual and inter-life involvement and evolution of various birds and animals. The inter-life involvement requires our understanding of nature's management, the environment and species, for our co-existence and their continuance for future generations.

I have had the honor and good fortune to meet and paint with a very large number of outstanding fellow artists including Carl Bauer in high school, David Hagerbaumer, Connie Schwiering, Robert Lougheed, John Clymer and Bob Kuhn. Just a few noted here, but excluding many who were influential, but deceased. I wish to thank Bill and Joffa Kerr for establishing an internationally recognized collection of animal and other subject art and sharing them with us all. Heartfelt thanks to my parents, Clark and Jean McHuron, my wife, Linda, and a large variety of others who have helped along the way.

I do hope you enjoy our mutual interpretations within these pages.

Greg McHuron
Jackson Hole

Greg McHuron is a most accomplished and versatile artist. He is also a teacher, a tough survivor and an inspiration to his peers. I delight in having him as a friend and now as a collaborator. I admire Greg for the dedication, artistry, inspiration and toughness he has brought to all of his works all of his life. I appreciate, as does he, the unwavering support his wife, Linda, provides.

I've appended a few words inspired by Greg's paintings on each of the birds featured. This book is an art book, not a field guide, yet because some of the birds may not be familiar even to experienced bird watchers, they may be useful.

My introduction to birds came rather late for a bird watcher today. Not that my wife and some friends hadn't tried to interest me in them. Fortunately for me, they succeeded and, importantly for me, they were as interested in the life histories and behaviors of the breeds as in their identification. Once enlightened, I soon found birds to be of endless interest. Now I've found birds in art in a different and entirely mind-exploding way: birds in their habitats as visualized by artists such as Greg McHuron, as if there are any artists just like Greg. It's yet another facet to the joy of watching birds and learning about them.

Greg McHuron and I invite you into the worlds of sage and scree as we see them.

I miss having my muse, Meg Raynes, to consult.

Bert Raynes
Jackson Hole

ACKNOWLEDGMENTS

We sincerely appreciate the hours of proofreading, copy editing and computer time by Stuart Carlton, Robin Christensen, Richard Collister, Jennifer Dorsey, Walt Farmer, Ron Gessler, Anna Goudet, Jan Hayse, Thomas Hahn, Mary Lohuis, James McNutt, Marlene Merrill, Adam Meyer, Susan Patla, Pamela Periconi, Joseph Piccoli, Larry Rieser, Sharon Rudd, Carol Schneebeck and Zeenie Scholz.

Garth Dowling converted the paintings to digits. Steven Epstein created the book design through many versions. Peter Ward, starting with the original text and paintings, skillfully organized the many processes necessary to produce the book.

We especially thank Charlie Craighead, Katy Duffy, Adam Harris, Tom Mangelsen, James McNutt, Thomas Quinn and Tony White for thoughtful reviews.

We hope we haven't inadvertently overlooked anyone.

INTRODUCTION

Birds have evolved to occupy or use just about every ecological habitat on Earth, including some places humans cannot conceive of as being either conducive or hospitable to bird life.

Bird watchers, in turn, have adapted and now practice their hobby in every habitat, on every continent — from tundra to tropics, even across vast oceans.

But one need not go to the ends of the Earth to find challenging terrain in which to watch birds. For example, consider the two habitats attended to in this volume, sagebrush and scree. Both are extensive habitats in the American West.

Sagebrush plains once were seemingly as vast as the seas in the arid inland west of North America. A boundless expanse of sagebrush, shrubs, forbs and grasses. Now much reduced in size by cultivation, development and energy exploitation, there remain sagebrush expanses that are challenging places simply to walk through, let alone places to bird watch.

Scree is a term describing the sloping fields of loose rocks, ranging in size from gravel to giant boulders, at the base of mountain cliffs or foothills. Talus is another term in general use for this geological feature, as in "talus piles." Correspondingly, "scree slopes" is frequently used. Scree slopes at their respective angles of repose can be slippery, difficult and even dangerous just to stand erect upon, let alone bird watch — or paint — from.

Too bad sage and scree discourage exploration. A host of birds, animals, plants and insects can be found in their subtly beautiful confines, many of them unfamiliar to nature watchers.

This book is a presentation of some of Greg McHuron's provocative paintings. Birds are feathered most prominently in these images, but details abound in the accurate representation of the settings. Greg found that detailing the mammals tends to divert our attention from the birds and their habitats. Therefore, he chose to use silhouettes to remind us that these mammals are an integral part of the habitats of sage and scree.

BLACK-THROATED SPARROW

In those parts of our Southwest where predominant sagebrush gives way to desert shrubs (creosote bush, cacti, rabbitbrush) can be found the "desert sparrow," the black-throated sparrow. In contrast to the cryptically plumaged bird species often inhabiting sagebrush and desert habitats, the black-throated sparrow is pretty spiffy. Pale gray above, light gray below with a dramatic black throat and chest, plus a strikingly marked head. Adults have white facial stripes, one through the eye and one under the chin. The tail is black except for a thin white stripe on the outer edge of the lateral rectrices, the stiff feathers on the sides of the tail.

Despite the black-throated sparrow's rather bold plumage, it can be mistaken for some related species such as the sage sparrow, black-chinned sparrow and five-striped sparrow. It's even mistaken, as I will confess from experience, for a male house sparrow, a juvenile or an adult with worn feathers before molt.

In the summer dawn choruses of bird song in arid desert habitat, the black-throated sparrow's is distinctive and sweet. It begins with two short notes followed by a rapid, sustained trill.

The desert sparrow is unusual in that while it frequents water sources when they are available, it can metabolize water from insects and plants if necessary. Every bird species has evolved individual traits and strategies. After all, they've had all that time since the dinosaur age.

This painting depicts typical black-throated sparrow habitat and suggests another denizen, the badger.

BROWN THRASHER

A bird watcher cruising the "sagebrush sea" of North America will initially identify a thrasher by its silhouette: robin-like shape and size, long tail, decurved bill. She or he might simply register "sage thrasher." With experience, the bird watcher might want to take a confirming second look; the similar-appearing brown thrasher does wander from its usual range in the East clear over to the front range of the Rocky Mountains.

Brown thrashers, shown in this rendering, share other characteristics with sage thrashers. Each is a songster, celebrated for exuberant spring performances. Male brown thrashers choose a conspicuous perch, point their tails downward and deliver long arias of rapidly repeated phrases, often several times in succession. A most unexpected performance, except in the courtship season, brown thrashers are skulkers, seldom seen except briefly when running away into undergrowth to hide. During his brief season of song exposure, one brown thrasher was determined to have sung up to two thousand songs! That number includes courtship songs given sotto voce just around the nest.

Brown thrashers' upper parts are a bright rufous; under parts a streaked white, two wing bars and striking yellow eyes. They're most at home on the ground, running or walking, or flying low over shrubbery as depicted.

Tip: Brown thrashers are more likely to nest in riparian zones and in dense vegetation than will sage thrashers. Sage thrashers, as their common name suggests, prefer the sage habitat.

BURROWING OWL

It's probably the eyes.

Mostly, perhaps. Owls have forward-facing, immobile eyes. Unlike most birds. Owls perch in a vertical posture, are relatively big-headed, have flat faces with feathered facial disk outlines and a decurved beak that is out of their line of vision. As a result of these aspects, owls suggest to many of us ... us.

Moreover, those owl eyes blink with their upper lids, as do we, not with their lower lids, as do all the other birds.

However, if the burrowing owls in Greg McHuron's painting resemble people, those people must be comically solemn in appearance. Permanently surprised clowns at that. Burrowing owls habitually are abroad by day as well as night. Here, a mated pair stand on long legs upon a mound of Earth next to the entrance of their burrow. That burrow may or may not have been excavated by the owls, for they readily take over burrows made by prairie dogs, badgers or other ground dwellers, then modify them to their needs. The results, typically, are tunnels roughly five inches in diameter, perhaps five to ten feet long, lined with an impressive variety of materials: leftover insect, bird and mammal remains, horse or cow dung, if available, and always infested with fleas.

Burrowing owls have had a long relationship with prairie dogs in North America, relying on these mammals as a primary diet item, their burrows for nests and for safety when endangered. As prairie dog populations have been reduced, so have the owls' numbers. Prosaically, burrowing owls are small owls from nine to eleven inches in length standing on unusually long legs, and are barred and spotted brown with a prominent white chin stripe, round-headed and short-tailed. Voice is a rapid chatter by day and a mellow cooo at night. That description doesn't hint at some burrowing owl behavior. From an erect standing posture they may abruptly begin to bow and twist, stretch and turn about and then may abruptly scramble into their hole. Not recommended behavior for people.

CLIFF SWALLOW

Eight swallow species nest in the United States. All are long-winged, swift-flying, insectivorous birds that feed on the wing. They are often iridescent blue or greenish above and white, rufous or black below.

Five species have common names derived from their choices of nesting sites: cliff swallow, tree swallow, bank swallow, cave swallow and barn swallow.

Cliff swallows do nest on cliffs at high elevations, places they share with bighorn sheep and other animals of the scree environment. However, they also nest on man-made structures, houses and other buildings in a variety of habitats. When locally common on buildings, they may become unpopular. Concentrations of birds lead to concentrations of bird droppings. Cliff swallows construct rounded nests of mud and saliva, small marvels made by the birds scooping up small mouthfuls of suitable mud or clay and then plastering them together to fashion a hollow gourd-shaped nest attached to a suitable vertical surface. A single opening is provided.

Watching cliff swallows at places where the mud is found, it's impossible not to recognize and share the high level of excitement or agitation among them. Wings are elevated and flutter rapidly, and the birds' behavior seems almost frenzied. But perhaps it's simply exuberance.

Cliff swallows are five inches in length, have typically long pointed wings and square tails. Adults have white on their foreheads, red faces, orange rumps and iridescent blue-black backs.

Incidentally, cliff swallows are the well-known swallows that return from Argentina to the Mission San Juan Capistrano in California every March.

COMMON RAVEN

On bleak days in the high-elevation scree or in flat sage steppe, your avian companion — if any — will be a common raven beating its way across the sky, playing on a cold wind in an empty universe, soaring, gliding, dipping now and again, and watching you. Seeing everything beneath, evaluating, calculating.

On other days there may be pairs of ravens (yes, pairs; they do mate for life), playing, doing Immelmanns, rollovers, swoops, dives, all the while making some of up to sixty or so vocalizations and individual calls that ravens are known to make. Or foursomes will be performing intricate aerial ballets. Perhaps a large group intently going somewhere they somehow know about and need to be.

Common ravens are large, much larger than crows. Over two feet in length, all black, heavy beaked. Ravens resemble some hawks in flight with their alternate flapping then sailing on flat wings. The tail is wedge-shaped.

The proper name for this large, black songbird is "common raven," but ravens are anything but common in their intelligence, behavior and ability to learn. They, and their cousin, the American crow, have the largest cerebral hemispheres, relative to body size, of any bird. A raven has the same brain-size-to-body-size as does a chimpanzee. Ravens learn quickly; they solve problems they encounter; they possess long-term memory; and they know how to play. To indulge in recognizable play is a sure sign of intelligence as well as an indication of a creature's success in survival skills.

Think of the common raven as the Can-Do Bird. Ravens can eat almost everything, hunt or scavenge, out-fly almost every other bird, live at high elevations in forest and in open country ... I haven't seen any swim, but I wouldn't put it past them.

Ferruginous Hawk

In many a Western movie and in innumerable television commercials, if the script calls for the penetrating cry of a bird to accompany the glimpse of one circling in an empty sky over a desolate treeless landscape, it's the red-tailed hawk's harsh scream that is heard. The bird shown could be a habitually silent vulture, an eagle or raven; no matter, the red-tailed hawk is heard. One could conclude it's the sole big hawk of the West.

Nay, not so. In the vast stretches of the sparsely treed, arid open country of the Interior West of North America, the iconic soaring hawk is the ferruginous hawk.

The ferruginous hawk is the biggest buteo of this habitat, even suggesting a golden eagle by its size and by some of its habits. Big-headed, burly-chested, with long, broad wings, it will sometimes cruise at low levels to flush or surprise prey. At other times it will soar at high altitudes searching for prairie dogs, ground squirrels, snakes and small birds. Moreover, it frequently sits on the ground to hunt, ignoring an opportunity afforded by some elevated perch.

Ferruginous hawks are not silent. Noisy, in fact, particularly around their nests. Their alarm cry, though harsh, is the softest of all the buteos, and pensive. Not good enough for the movies.

GOLDEN EAGLE

Who hasn't dreamed of flying? The freedom to flap your arms and simply lift off and escape gravity. To soar, to dive, to glide. Soaring effortlessly while also possessing the eyesight of a golden eagle with its mastery of the air and its variables. With its apparent freedom of choice. To see into far distances while capable of spotting the slightest movement of a marmot or rabbit from a great height.

Swell. But that's just a small part of a golden eagle's existence. The constant is struggle. Struggle from that moment when, after hours of effort and persistence, a chick emerges from its eggshell. Two chicks are born, but usually only the older, larger one survives, winning the contest for food brought by its parents. Then continues the daily struggle every wild creature must face and overcome each day, simply to exist.

Golden eagles prefer high places where they hunt marmots, hares, mice, birds, even foxes, young deer and pronghorn. When hunting fails, they will scavenge on carrion or attempt to take prey they would ordinarily judge to be too large and fierce to attack (even wolverines!). In this painting, artist McHuron depicts a golden eagle in its prime. Notice the massive beak, the golden wash on head and neck, massively broad great wings, and outsized talons. Since it is an adult, this bird has survived its daily struggles for at least five years. It may live, wild and free, for another twenty-five years.

So, in your dream of being able to fly, run and flap, lift off and soar, imagine yourself as a golden eagle. Master of the sky.

GREATER SAGE-GROUSE

Two hundred years ago, Lewis and Clark and the Corps of Discovery came upon their "cock of the plains" — the greater sage-grouse. The large, striking wildfowl thrived in what's been described as a sagebrush sea. They still live there; they must, for they are utterly dependent on sagebrush habitat.

Today, the sagebrush sea has been drastically reduced in overall size and, perhaps of far greater significance, is being largely fragmented into isolated segments.

In the 1800s, flocks of sage grouse would darken the sky. Some fifty percent habitat loss and its fragmentation has now reduced sage grouse to about eight percent of estimated historic numbers. There is legitimate concern that this species could go the way of other former North American birds, such as the passenger pigeon, Carolina parakeet and Eskimo curlew. Another species of sage grouse, the Gunnison sage-grouse, recognized only in the 1990s, is in serious danger of imminent extirpation.

Nonetheless, greater sage-grouse remain locally common and a game bird hunted in many parts of the Inland West. They're big, chicken-like birds considered by some to be tasty. Males approach the size of a small turkey, females notably smaller. Overall a dark brownish with a black belly. Males also have a dark black throat and bill. Distinctive long, pointed, mottled tails. Greater sage-grouse are known, along with certain related species, for exaggerated mating displays on traditional grounds known as leks (an assembly area where grouse, or any other animals, conduct display and courtship behavior).

Male sage grouse gather on these leks in early spring to perform. They fan their pointed tail feathers, erect their head plumes and strut their stuff, inflating and deflating prominent breast sacs with accompanying plops, swishing their wings and swaggering. Females come to the leks to size up and choose a male, copulate and leave to nest on their own and raise their broods.

It's like a scene from a popular bar at closing time.

GREEN-TAILED TOWHEE

For such a brightly plumaged bird, a green-tailed towhee can be difficult to find and hard to identify. Just how it accomplished this isn't entirely clear; its color pattern doesn't suggest cryptic coloration. (Cryptic coloration serves to conceal, distract or obscure. Think camouflage.) Maybe it's that vertical stripe on the towhee's face.

Study Greg's portraits of this bird of the interior Mountain West. A mere six inches long, a rufous crown, a white throat in contrast to olive-greenish upper parts; has a loud, sprightly song in breeding season, often given from the topmost perch of a sagebrush, shrub or small tree. Green-tailed towhees also have a distinctive call, a catlike mewing sound. All this and yet locating the bird in the field can be challenging.

One explanation may be the green-tailed towhee "rodent run." In the mid-1900s, a Colorado chap, thinking he was gunning down a chipmunk, shot a green-tailed towhee by mistake. Subsequently, nature observers recognized that these towhees, when disturbed by a potential predator, habitually drop down from their nests, normally a short distance, and with their tails held erect, run directly from the area to distract the intruder. The "rodent run" is unlike this bird's normal hop-and-pause locomotion. In doing so, the green tail can strongly resemble a chipmunk, distracting some predators.

However, on an early spring morning when a green-tailed towhee flies to some conspicuous perch, stands boldly in a shaft of sunlight and delivers his buzzy, finch-like declarations, he's unmistakable. A knockout.

HORNED LARK

Charming little couple, isn't it?

Horned larks. Small. Brown. Ground birds. Pretty spiffy male — the brighter-plumaged one with his tiny "horns." Female birds, generally, are less colorful than their mates so as to attract less attention from predators when sitting on eggs or caring for young. (Nature, being creative and adventurous, evolved a few bird species that reverse this almost universal arrangement. In these instances, the males attend the eggs and nests, and the females have the brighter plumage and mess around. Phalaropes are examples.)

Horned larks are gregarious, spending most of their lives in groups and flocks, preferring open ground, prairies characterized by shorter grasses and forbs. The more barren the habitat to our eye, the better it seems for the bird.

When horned larks pair off in their spring breeding season, the male performs a display that earns the name "lark." He flies silently to respectable heights, sometimes hundreds of feet above, then repeats his high-pitched ringing boastful song over and over, sometimes for several minutes, as he flies in tight circles, then silently speeds back to ground. Pleasant to our ears; effective, too, for horned larks are widespread and abundant in open habitats in North America.

Gregory i. M Hurow

LOGGERHEAD SHRIKE

To paraphrase a truly old saw, the loggerhead shrike must be the work product of a committee.

The loggerhead shrike is a songbird that reminds of a raptor, from its accipiter-like shape to its resemblance to a mimic thrush (the northern mockingbird), and to its reliance on hunting of prey ranging from small birds and small mammals to a variety of insects. It hunts from an elevated perch and kills its prey using its hooked bill. A songbird raptor. A raptor songbird.

The loggerhead shrike's bill is of special interest. One group of birds of prey, the falcons, has a feature of its bills called the "tomial tooth." The tomial tooth is a sharp, downward-pointing projection on falcons' upper mandible that in turn fits into a notch in the lower mandible. The tomial tooth's purpose is to bite through the cervical vertebrae of its prey and sever its spinal column. (Soaring hawks, eagles and accipiters kill with their powerful toes and talons.) The only birds other than falcons that have the tomial tooth are shrikes.

Lacking the strong feet and talons of a bird of prey, a shrike will habitually impale its kill on a thorn, a twig or a barb of fencing, etc., to secure it when feeding. This has earned shrikes the moniker "butcherbird," after the sight of carcasses hanging on hooks in a butcher's cooler.

As in mockingbirds, a shrike's plumage is one of distinctly defined blacks, grays and whites. Shrikes are about nine inches in length and have outsized heads. The shrike has a black line through the eye, a mark the mockingbird lacks. Voice is harsh, a bit like a mockingbird.

The source of the shrike's common English name is not known. "Shrike" may be a confusion with "shriek," for Europe has a shrike look-alike that really does shriek nightly. "Loggerhead" in some biological writings suggests big-headed. But this is speculation; maybe there was some conceited taxonomist nicknamed Loggerhead. Let's hope.

LONG-BILLED CURLEW

A two-foot bird with a three-foot wingspan, an outlandish down-curved, sickle-shaped bill, flashing dark cinnamon under wings and piercing cries commands attention.

Long-billed curlews are shorebirds that prefer to breed on dry open prairies in their remaining habitat in the interior American West, albeit often close to a pond or watercourse. Even in winter — although many long-billed curlews migrate to seashores, salt marshes and mudflats — most prefer fields and prairie.

Despite the long-billed curlew's large size (it is the largest of North American shorebirds), its overall yellowish-brown plumage helps camouflage the bird even when in open terrain. Detection, however, is at times easy; long-billed curlews are noisy birds. Their calls are variously interpreted as piercing, plaintive, musical, fluting, delightful. Always loud. A characteristic rising and falling curl-e-e-e-u-u-call note has suggested its common name. There's also a rapid kU-U-U-U and a rising cur-lee.

The long-billed curlew reaches a height of two feet on dark legs and sports a long, thin, down-curved bill that is dark at its droplet-shaped tip, shading to a flesh tone at its base. This crescent-shaped bill can be eight inches long.

Once abundant, the "sicklebill" is now uncommon. Around the turn of the last century, its large size, its easy decoying by imitating its calls, its unfortunate habit of attempting to investigate the cries of a wounded companion, and its palatability, led to its drastic decline. Overhunting, along with habitat loss as land was given over to agriculture, almost extirpated the species. Count yourself fortunate to see long-billed curlews in the wild.

MOUNTAIN BLUEBIRD

Early in the 20th century, one popular common name for one of the continent's blue birds was "azure bluebird."

Kind of too bad it didn't stick. What an appropriate term for the delightful coloration of this thrush.

Of course, there's turquoise, sky blue, lapus lazuli and ... blue.

Bluebirds — there are three recognized species in North America — are well-known not just for their colors, but also for their habit of being an early spring migrant. The mountain bluebird, the bird portrayed here, is expected in some parts of the western United States to return when snow still covers the Earth. Then these insectivorous birds must rely upon native fruits and berries remaining on various shrubs and trees and upon various insects that emerge on some late winter days. This male mountain bluebird (males return before females do) is perched on a last season's mullein, searching for anything to eat.

The male mountain bluebird is overall blue. A deeper blue above, paler (azure) below, shading to an almost white. Females are brownish with blue on tail and wings. It's a small thrush that prefers open country with some trees.

Mountain bluebirds and their cousins, the eastern bluebird and the western bluebird (makes one yearn for "azure," doesn't it?), will nest near human habitation and will accept manmade nest boxes if in appropriate locations. The required nest-box hole for mountain bluebird occupation is one-sixteenth of an inch larger in diameter than holes for its relatives; it's that broad-shouldered Western tradition, don't you know.

Smile, pardner.

MOURNING DOVE

This fine watercolor of mourning doves could be titled "Fast Flyers." For indeed they are: just consider their form, which speaks descriptively of aeronautical evolution, with long pointed wings, relatively slim streamlined body, long, tapered, pointed, rudder-like tail.

This is the ubiquitous dove of North America, ranging widely from southeast Alaska, southern Canada to South America. So abundant that it often goes unremarked or would be if not for its familiar, pervasively lugubrious cooing voice: cooah, coo, coo, coo. Which is to say, mournful.

Mourning doves nod their heads as they walk. A foot-long brown bird with a pointed tail adorned with outer white spots. Their wings make an arresting sound, particularly as the bird bursts into flight. And, uniquely among doves and pigeons, they produce a "crop milk" with which to feed their young. Crop milk is a secretion produced in the lining of the crops of doves and pigeons, and regurgitated to feed nestlings. It resembles mammal milk, composed of fat and protein, rich in vitamins A and B.

Of interest: Doves and related pigeons are able to drink without raising their heads. Almost all other bird species cannot; they must dip their bills into water and raise their heads to allow the water to flow down their throats.

PEREGRINE FALCON AND CLARK'S NUTCRACKER

He's gaining on 'em.

Doesn't mean the pursuing peregrine falcon will seize one of the fleeing Clark's nutcrackers in the next instant; predators never succeed in every pursuit. Far from it; it's never a given outcome for each participant, this life-and-death moment.

Yet, don't bet against it. The nutcrackers are in dire peril. Peregrine falcons make their living almost exclusively by killing and eating other birds. Their superior aerial skills enable them to chase down birds in flight, birds ranging in size and maneuverability from swallows and swifts to cranes and herons. Their oversize feet — they were once called the "great-footed hawk" — are capable of delivering a knockout blow or administering an instantaneous lethal grip.

The peregrine falcon is the better known of these two species, for it is found worldwide primarily in Arctic and temperate climes. Better known, yes, but never common; top-of-the-food-chain wild animals are never abundant.

Peregrine falcons are almost crow-size, have long pointed wings, slate-colored backs, whitish breasts and a distinctive facial pattern featuring a thick, dark mustache mark. Fast, powerful, deadly and unforgettable.

Clark's nutcrackers are restricted in their range to higher elevations in the coniferous forests of western North America. They resemble small crows except for the large white patches in their black wings and tails. In years past, they were called "Clark's Crow" as an honor to William Clark, who first collected and made a preliminary description of this species during the epic Lewis and Clark Expedition. That was on August 22, 1805, along the Salmon River in present-day Idaho. He initially thought they were woodpeckers, but Meriwether Lewis corrected the identification the next May while in the Bitterroot Mountains.

Greg McHuron has captured an encounter between the two species in a remote high-mountain habitat explored by Lewis and Clark on behalf of a then-much-smaller United States.

PIPIT

These birds are sometimes referred to as "small, earth-toned avifauna." In particular, little brown jobs of high-altitude alpine barrens: American (water) pipits.

Yes, small and brown, sparrow-sized and -shaped, inhabitants of open country — rocky mountain slopes in summer, open agricultural expanses in winter. American pipits walk, not hop, habitually bobbing their tails. The tail sports white outer feathers, as do the tails of a number of other ground-dwelling birds that during some seasons flock together: meadowlarks, dark-eyed juncos, others. It is presumed these white feathers serve both as signals to others of their kind and also to deceive predators.

Owing to a dearth of elevated perches in their habitat, many open-country bird species often sing their mating songs aloft. The male pipit's repetitious, ringing trill accelerates as he spirals down with tail spread, stopping abruptly once he lands. But that is in spring. In this scene, a grizzly bear has ascended a high-mountain scree slope somewhere in the Northern Rockies in late summer to feast on army cutworm moths. These insects occur in such number in some particular locations and in some years as to provide a significant source of protein for the bears in their preparations for hibernation. The moths go there to mate and feed on alpine flower nectar, hiding under the rocks during the heat of day. Ultimately the moths return to the Great Plains before onset of winter.

By displacing and overturning rocks in their hunt, the bears disturb and expose the moths, some of which will take flight, becoming vulnerable to insectivorous birds. In this instance, a little flock of American pipits.

An ordinary extraordinary juxtaposition of natural events.

Predator and prey. The gray-crowned rosy finches brought to life in this painting should not be, and most likely are not, confident they are immune to attack from the prairie falcon flying in the opposite direction. The prairie falcon has, of course, seen the little finch flock, for it makes its living primarily by preying on flocking birds. Only when habitually flocking birds are relatively solitary in their nesting and breeding season do prairie falcons rely instead primarily on ground squirrels.

This particular falcon is making a foray into the higher mountain elevations where rosy finches prefer to nest. As its common name suggests, the prairie falcon generally is found in America's West in open country and foothills, but as with other birds of prey—and indeed all predators — they are opportunistic hunters. This individual has headed into the higher mountain elevations, perhaps in late summer when prairie falcons regularly visit these areas to look for flocking rosy finches and other mountain birds.

Prairie falcons are large hawks, nearly crow-size. Overall brown except for a white eyebrow and a black-brown "mustache." Seen from underneath, they have distinctive blackish wing pits.

Gray-crowned rosy finch. At the whim of professional ornithologists, rosy finches have at times been "lumped" generally as rosy finches, or "split." When lumped, they're all rosy finches. When split, each rosy gets it due: gray-crowned rosy finch, black rosy finch and brown-capped rosy finch. The splitters presently prevail; artist McHuron illustrates here the gray-crowned rosy finch. Social in winter, mixed flocks wander in search of food, remaining at about 4,500-feet elevation.

Of interest: An experienced observer recently documented an instance in which a flock of white-crowned sparrows reacted to the alarm call of a ground squirrel by fleeing to safety in an evergreen tree just as a frustrated prairie falcon banked away. Since both small birds and rodents are favored prey items for this falcon, a kind of interspecies communication cannot be discounted.

(Now, there's a potential Ph.D. topic.)

Rock Wren

In western North America are both extensive and small expanses of open, sunny, steep and rocky slopes with scattered boulders and rocks and not much vegetation.

Mountainsides, canyons, cliffs, taluses and loose pebbly rocks. Should you find yourself in one of these scenic places in summer months as a hiker, climber or bird watcher, you might not have many animal companions. A pika, perhaps as suggested here, a common raven cruising by, maybe a bighorn sheep, a skunk, a marmot.

If lucky, a rock wren. If luckier still, you may find its nest.

Some rock wrens construct what we humans construe anthropomorphically as a "pathway" leading to nests hidden in a crevice or hole on a shelf of an exposed rock surface. Small, flat stones are primarily used for the nest or for the pathway, but pebbles and other small objects may be utilized. One obsessed observer recorded the small natural and manmade objects used by an equally obsessed rock wren in one nest: 1,665 items.

The nest itself consisted of grasses, weed stems and a few feathers. We're talking here of a lot of effort for a small bird, but you know what love can make one do.

I know of no other Northern American bird that has a corresponding nesting behavior. Rock wrens are only about six inches in length, but they have a bigger voice than that; they are loud. Perhaps it's because they have so much empty space to fill as they perch on a rock high up on some mountain, bounce up and down and hold forth. A repeated, somewhat harsh tikeer. A relatively long-billed grayish-brown wren with a lightly streaked breast, a rusty rump and buffy tail corners.

Greg McHuron's rock wren is shown in early summer, in a typical pose, about to do his "knee bends" and announce himself and his real estate. Come to me, my lovely.

Sage Sparrow

Its scientific name, *Amphispiza belli*, doesn't come trippingly to most tongues, particularly as an announcement in the field of a bird sighting. Few nonprofessional bird watchers would utter it — although I notice even beginning botanists tend to wallow happily in the Latin and Greek identifications — for simple bird watchers are most likely never to have learned the scientific names. Oh well. They are almost sure to call out "Sage sparrow." There might be a note of triumph and satisfaction in the whisper or shout "Sage sparrow, two o'clock, in the tallest sagebrush."

Despite the sage sparrow's handsome plumage — gray brown, dark narrow mustache, longish dark tail, clean white breast adorned with a single black medallion — it can be challenging to spot. It has a habit of sitting motionless, imitating a part of its perch but betrayed by its twitching tail. If alarmed or about to search for food, it drops to the ground and runs about. Much of its time is spent on the ground as it seeks escape or its food: insects, spiders, weed seeds and plants. As with other ground-dwelling sparrows or their allies, it can zip speedily between sheltering bushes.

A sage sparrow also raises its tail when running, holding it at about an angle of 45 degrees, perhaps to mimic a mouse or other small animal.

In some parts of the sage sparrow's breeding range, which is from Wyoming west to California, Oregon, Washington and south into Mexico, at appropriate seasons its high-pitched rather mellow song is somewhat weak but also rather sweet.

In winter months, sage sparrows may gather in small flocks. It is not a good field mark — not an outstanding color or shape or mark or combination of some of these that help identify a species — but the two outer tail feathers of this sparrow are a light buff, not quite as prominent as those on most open-country land birds that also flick them.

This bird prefers the tallest sage and other shrubs in the habitat. A pretty subtle field mark, but perhaps helpful at some times in their identification.

SHORT-EARED OWL

The bulky shape and solemn visage belie the buoyant aerodynamic capabilities of this otherwise ground-dwelling, crow-size, short-eared owl. When hunting, this predator flies low over open ground, alternately flapping languidly then sailing, making abrupt turns, hovering for up to half a minute before plunging to Earth to snatch a mouse or vole or bird. In these maneuvers the owl can be confused with a harrier, whose quartering hunt patterns are similar, but its overall tawny brown color, short tail and lack of the hawk's white rump are distinctive.

Courtship flight is exuberant.

While the female watches from the ground, the suitor spirals high, to a thousand feet perhaps, while repeatedly calling whoot, whoot, whoot. The flight becomes level but erratic with swoops, dives and climbs, the wingtips slapping together under the bird's body, producing a sharp, clapping noise. This appeal may last ten minutes or more, culminating in rollovers, somersaults and a free fall to ground accompanied with wing clapping and piercing cries. What female can resist?

Nests are on or under the ground in an improvised or abandoned animal burrow. Occasionally, vegetation hides the entrance. The presence of this owl — it is widespread in North America — is usually made known as it habitually hunts by day or when one is accidentally stumbled upon in the field.

TOWNSEND'S SOLITAIRE

This bird resembles flycatchers and often behaves as flycatchers do, but it isn't one. It's patterned like a mockingbird, but isn't one. It often feeds the way a bluebird does, but isn't that one either. It looks like a smaller, slimmer, gray robin with a pleasing song, and its juveniles are heavily spotted; all that gets close to its true identity. The Townsend's solitaire is a thrush, but it took early ornithologists and taxonomists quite a while to establish its place in the hierarchy of bird families.

The Townsend's solitaire has a thin eye-ring, white outer tail feathers and buff wing patches on an eight-inch drab gray body — field marks that can be subtle and overlooked. A quick glance suggests a female mountain bluebird, but not the song. Townsend's solitaire's song is loud, melodious, lengthy and suggestive of the songs of thrushes and also finches. It is given at appropriate times in summer, fall and early winter. And unlike other bird species, Townsend's solitaires of both sexes sing the same song and give four identical, distinctive call notes.

The Townsend's solitaire is a bird of the high mountains, of open forests and steep slopes, leaving only in winter to find juniper berries. Indeed, rather solitary except when nesting and when an exceptionally generous berry crop in a particular locale attracts a gathering of them.

A gentle, retiring bird, except in defense of its nest. Be especially pleased when you recognize one. The first specimen was collected by the pioneer naturalist, James Kirk Townsend (1801-51), for whom it is appropriately named. It was identified as a solitaire by John James Audubon.

VESPER SPARROW

Let's face it: There's a slew of small brownish sparrows and allied bird species in North America. A dozen species can be found nesting in sage and its environs: chipping, Brewer's, vesper, lark, black-throated, sage, Savannah, grasshopper, fox, song, Lincoln's and white-crowned sparrow.

A couple of these sparrows' names suggest field marks that would help a hapless bird watcher in his identifications, but most don't. Take the vesper sparrow shown here. Its common name won't help. It was John Burroughs, an early American literary naturalist and essayist important to the evolution from wanton slaughter of wildlife to their conservation, who in the late 1870s wrote that this sparrow sings most melodiously at eventide. Vespers.

But in fact, this large sparrow sings its sweet song, introduced by two to four clear opening notes followed by musical trills, from morning to night in its breeding season. Nevertheless, the common name has stuck.

Vesper sparrows display white outer tail feathers in flight. So do other birds of open sage country. Horned larks, lark sparrows, longspurs, even the much larger meadowlarks. A tip: Vesper sparrows have a white eye-ring these other birds lack. All have pleasant songs, none sweeter than that of the vesper sparrow.

WESTERN MEADOWLARK

Two meadowlark species occur over a large area of North America. The western meadowlark, depicted here, and an outwardly similar species. It would take an experienced bird watcher — or an artist — to distinguish one from the other in the field but for their different voices and location.

The western meadowlark's songs, delivered in flight or when perched, are often variously described as flutelike, clear, carrying — all thirty of them. It's a yodeler and may vocalize at all hours and weather conditions and seasons.

The eastern meadowlark's voice is softer, less musical and less varied, consisting of two slurred whistles.

Each species is nine inches in length, plump, brown above with black streaks, brilliant yellow below with a conspicuous black gorget. Each has large, painted bills and large white-tipped tail feathers that are displayed in flight and flicked as the meadowlarks walk on long legs. They're not larks but instead are closely related to other blackbirds with more pleasant voices.

The male western meadowlark sings, as I mentioned, persistently. Perhaps it's because he may have two or three females he's courted and mated with and he must keep other males at bay. Everything's a trade-off.

A couple of interesting facts:

The western meadowlark is the state bird of six western states: Wyoming, Nebraska, Kansas, North Dakota, Oregon and Montana. No state calls the eastern meadowlark its state bird.

Lewis and Clark, splendid lads they, recognized the western meadowlark during their epic journey as different from the outwardly identical ones they were familiar with in the then-seventeen United States. It took forty years and John James Audubon to rediscover the species. It was then given the specific species name *neglecta*.

Gregory i McHuron ©

WHITE-TAILED PTARMIGAN

Here are birds of extreme rocky tundra. Alpine/Arctic life zone. Way up there.

White-tailed ptarmigan (TAR-mi-gan). Of three ptarmigan species endemic in North America, this is the only one found anywhere south of Canada. Even there it inhabits only a few high-mountain sites in the United States in harsh environmental conditions where only a few equally hardy plants (spruce, willows, flowering forbs) can also survive.

These ground-dwelling smallest of all grouse remain capable of accommodating frigid temperatures and life at tree line or above without migrating. For protection against predators, they molt to match their surroundings, from mottled brown backs, breasts and heads, and feathered feet in warmer months to all white in winter. All white except for black eyes and beaks. Their tails are, as the name implies, always white.

White-tailed ptarmigan are only a foot long and weigh less than a pound. They subsist on willow and forbs in spring and summer but primarily on willow buds in winter. They persist in winter by roosting under the snow.

Oh, yes. A bit of trivia you probably could joyfully do without knowing: In winter, a white-tailed ptarmigan defecates an average of forty-nine times overnight.

Winter nights are long.

WHITE-THROATED SWIFT

The white-throated swift is aptly named. It flies very swiftly, and it does have a white throat field mark that extends down a black belly.

Wherever it is found, from isolated high-elevation cliffs to a new adaptation — urban freeway interchange structures and even tall buildings — it seems to be almost constantly airborne. White-throated swifts hunt their insect prey and eat while on the wing. They court and even mate while airborne, spiraling toward the ground before separating only when about to crash. Recently it was discovered that they even take naps while in flight.

White-throated swifts have a six-inch cigar-shaped body with crescent-shaped wings that span fourteen inches and a short, notched tail. Black on upper parts, black belly and sides of breast along with isolated white spots on flank — a resemblance to violet-green swallows. Swallows have longer tails and broader wings than swifts do. The swift's call, given often, is an excited fee feee feee fee. Both these swifts and violet-green swallows often associate at colonial nesting sites.

All North American swifts — white-throated, Vaux's, chimney and black — beat their wings so rapidly that they appear to "twinkle" and even beat alternately — an illusion. When the birds soar, their wings are held in a bowed position.

About Greg McHuron

Greg McHuron is a plein-air painter working in oil and watercolor/gouache. He primarily paints wildlife and landscapes throughout the United States and Canada. He was born in 1945 in Syracuse, New York, and raised in Colorado, Wyoming, Alaska and California. He always wanted to be an artist and began sketching at an early age.

Greg graduated from Oregon State University in 1968 with a bachelor's degree in arts as well as being schooled in forestry and fisheries and wildlife. After graduating, he worked as a designer and Art Director for an interior design firm before moving to Jackson to be close to the subjects he prefers to paint.

He has taught workshops, given demonstrations and participated in quick-draws for a variety of organizations including the Wyoming Artists Association, Wind River Artist Association, Scottsdale School of the Arts, The Lodge at Palisades, National Museum of Wildlife Art, CM Russell Show, Grand Teton National Park, Isle Royale National Park and Gates of the Arctic National Park and Preserve.

Greg travels extensively, explaining, "I prefer painting on location as much as possible en plein air as the drama and excitement that occurs all around me is difficult to re-create in a studio environment. When I paint the rapidly changing scenes, I put into each of them the feelings and excitement that I felt while watching the scene unfold. Years of watching, analyzing and learning from nature's school ground has helped me to understand the inter-relations between organic and inorganic entities and how different lighting, seasons and locations affect how they look and react. If I can capture that particular feeling, I know that those viewing my works will come to feel some of the emotions and excitement that motivated my wanting to record this particular fleeting moment."

Greg's painting trips have ranged from above the Arctic Circle at Selby Lake, Alaska, to boat trips along the coast of southeast Alaska and British Columbia, to the Queen Charlotte and Vancouver Islands, to the Okanagan Game Farm, British Columbia, to Banff and Jasper national parks, Alberta, to wilderness areas in Wyoming and Colorado, to the Colorado River through the Grand Canyon.

Greg spent several summers as Artist-In-Residence at Isle Royale and Glacier national parks. He has won awards from the National Museum of Wildlife Art in Jackson, Wyoming, the Rocky Mountain Plein Air Painter Association in Winter Park, Colorado, the Wild, Wild West Show in Scottsdale, Arizona, the Plein Air 2005 Show at the Arizona-Sonora Desert Museum in Tucson, Arizona, the Animal Kingdom Show VII at the Bennington Center for the Arts in Bennington, Vermont, and the Wind River Valley Show in Dubois, Wyoming. He was Artist of the Year of the Wyoming Artist Association in 1999, U.S. Representative to the Leighton Foundation Artist Retreat in Calgary, Alberta, Canada, in 1991, and Wyoming Wildlife Federation Stamp Winner in 1985.

About Bert Raynes

Bert Raynes became interested in nature observation rather late for a person now considered to be a naturalist. Already married and starting a career in chemical engineering, having no formal training in wildlife and their lives, he relied upon his wife, Meg, field studies, books and, luckily, associations with some exceptional biologists who befriended him and taught by example.

After a very successful career as a chemical engineer in New York and Ohio and a stint as president of the Cleveland Audubon Society, Bert and Meg retired to Jackson Hole in 1972, where they had spent summers for nearly 20 years. By 1976, he had founded the Jackson Hole Bird Club. Soon he began writing a weekly nature-based column for the *Jackson Hole News&Guide* that has been read eagerly by bird watchers and other lovers of nature for more than three decades.

Eager to share any knowledge he acquired, Raynes has written *Birds of Grand Teton and the Surrounding Area, Finding the Birds of Jackson Hole: A bird finding guide*, two pocket guides to birds of Jackson Hole and Yellowstone, *Curmudgeon Chronicles* and, with Tom Mangelsen, *Winter Wings: Birds of the Northern Rockies*. Recently, he inaugurated the Meg and Bert Raynes Wildlife Fund to encourage the documentation of wildlife by both professional and, especially, citizen naturalists.

Doubtless, Bert's main interest in nature has been birds. While he preached that watching birds can be done almost everywhere, he noticed that some promising bird habitats with difficult access got less attention. In particular, Raynes found that students in beginning birding classes tended to avoid scree slopes and attempting to cross expanses of sagebrush. Thus, birds that inhabit these ecosystems are lesser known. He has long thought that these birds should be better understood.

Separately and together, Meg and Bert Raynes have been recognized for their dedication to conservation and wildlife issues by the National Museum of Wildlife Art, the Wildlife Heritage Foundation, the Wyoming Chapter of the Wildlife Society, the Wyoming Game and Fish Department, the Jackson Hole Conservation Alliance and the Town of Jackson.

Glossary

Aria	An elaborate melody sung by a single source.	Plops	A sound like that of something dropping into water.
Brood	Young birds hatched or cared for at one time.	Plumage	The entire clothing of feathers of a bird.
Buteo	A hawk with broad wings and soaring flight.	Rectrices	The main feathers of a bird's tail.
Cryptic	A plumage pattern and coloration that conceal a bird from predators.	Riparian	Relating to the bank of a natural watercourse, or lake, or tidewater.
Decurved	Curved downward.	Rufous	Reddish.
Extirpate	To wipe out completely.	Sage	(Or sagebrush) Various kinds of composite aromatic plants that once covered vast tracts of alkaline plains in the western U.S.
Ferruginous	Resembling iron rust in color.		
Forb	An herb other than grass.	Scree	An accumulation of loose stones or rocky debris lying on a slope or at the base of a hill or cliff (also talus).
Gorget	An ornamental collar.		
Immelmann	A turn in which an airplane or bird in flight first makes a half-loop and then rolls half of a complete turn.	Sotto Voce	Very softly.
		Vespers	Melodies sung in the late afternoon.
Lek	An assembly area where animals, especially grouse, conduct display and courtship behavior.		
Molt	To shed feathers, hair, antlers, etc. periodically.		
Mullein	A woody-leaved herb of the figwort family (also mullen).		